Delivering Excellence: How To Give Presentations That Make A Difference

Presentation techniques that will transform a speech into a memorable event

"Practical, proven techniques that will help you to make your next speech a success"

Dr. Jim Anderson

Published by:
Blue Elephant Consulting
Tampa, Florida

Copyright © 2013 by Dr. Jim Anderson

All rights reserved. No part of this book may be reproduced of transmitted in any form or by any means, electronic or mechanical, including photocopying, recording or by any information storage and retrieval system without written permission of the publisher, except for inclusion of brief quotations in a review.

Printed in the United States of America

Library of Congress Control Number: 2016916423

ISBN-13: 978-1539173618
ISBN-10: 1539173615

Warning – Disclaimer

The purpose of this book is to educate and entertain. This book does not promise or guarantee that anyone following the ideas, tips, suggestions, techniques or strategies will be hired. It is the discretion of employers if you will or will not be hired. The author, publisher and distributor(s) shall have neither liability nor responsibility to anyone with respect to any loss or damage caused, or alleged to be caused, directly or indirectly by the information contained in this book.

Recent Books By The Author

Product Management

- How To Create A Successful Product That Customers Will Want: Techniques For Product Managers To Boost Product Sales And Increase Customer Satisfaction

- What Product Managers Need To Know About World-Class Product Development: How Product Managers Can Create Successful Products

Public Speaking

- Tools Speakers Need In Order To Give The Perfect Speech: What tools to use to create your next speech so that your message will be remembered forever!

- How To Create A Speech That Will Be Remembered

CIO Skills

- Becoming A Powerful And Effective Leader: Tips And Techniques That IT Managers Can Use In Order To Develop Leadership Skills

- CIO Secrets For Growing Innovation: Tips And Techniques For CIOs To Use In Order To Make Innovation Happen In Their IT Department

IT Manager Skills

- Save Yourself, Save Your Job – How To Manage Your IT Career: Secrets That IT Managers Can Use In Order To Have A Successful Career

- Growing Your CIO Career: How CIOs Can Work With The Entire Company In Order To Be Successful

Negotiating

- Take No Prisoners In Your Next Negotiation: How To Start A Negotiation In Order To Get The Best Possible Outcome

- Learn How To Signal In Your Next Negotiation: How To Develop The Skill Of Effective Signaling In A Negotiation In Order To Get The Best Possible Outcome

Note: See a complete list of books by Dr. Jim Anderson at the back of this book.

Acknowledgements

Any book like this one is the result of years of real-world work experience. In my over 25 years of working for 7 different firms, I have met countless fantastic people and I've been mentored by some truly exceptional ones. Although I've probably forgotten some of the people who made me the person that I am today, here is my attempt to finally give them the recognition that they so truly deserve:

- Thomas P. Anderson
- Art Puett
- Bobbi Marshall
- Bob Boggs

Dr. Jim Anderson

This book is dedicated to my wife Lori. None of this would have been possible without her love and support.

Thanks for the best years of my life (so far)...!

Table Of Contents

HOW TO DELIVER EXCELLENCE IN YOUR NEXT SPEECH 8

ABOUT THE AUTHOR 10

CHAPTER 1: PRESENTATION CHALLENGE: HOW TO SUCCESSFULLY TALK TO TEENS – AND SURVIVE! 15

CHAPTER 2: WHAT TO DO WHEN YOU SAY THE WRONG THING DURING A PRESENTATION 19

CHAPTER 3: HOW TO PREPARE YOUR VOICE FOR YOUR NEXT PRESENTATION 23

CHAPTER 4: IT'S ALL ABOUT THE NONVERBAL, PRESENTER 27

CHAPTER 5: HOW PRESENTERS CAN GIVE A TOAST WITHOUT TOASTING A RELATIONSHIP 31

CHAPTER 6: D.O.A.: WHY PRESENTERS HATE BAD INTRODUCTIONS 35

CHAPTER 7: REAL LIFE SPEECHES: GEORGE HALVORSON, CEO OF KAISER FOUNDATION HEALTH PLAN, INC. 39

CHAPTER 8: REAL LIFE SPEECHES: ALAN GREENSPAN GIVES A KEYNOTE 43

CHAPTER 9: DENNIS QUAID GIVES A KEYNOTE SPEECH – REAL LIFE SPEECHES 48

CHAPTER 10: CAN YOU HEAR ME NOW IS WHAT PRESENTERS NEED TO KNOW 52

CHAPTER 11: HANDLING HECKLERS: 5 WAYS THAT PRESENTERS CAN RESTORE ORDER 56

CHAPTER 12: SPEAKING POWER: HOW TO GET IT, HOW TO USE IT .. 62

How To Deliver Excellence In Your Next Speech

So why do we give speeches? I mean, talk about an effort! When you agree to give a speech all of a sudden you realize that you've signed yourself up to pick what you want to talk about, do whatever research is required, actually write the speech, and then spend a great deal of time practicing how you are going to say it. What's the purpose of all of this?

It turns out that the purpose is actually quite simple – we want our next presentation to make a difference. No matter if we've agreed to talk with teens, if we've screwed up and said the wrong thing, or if we're not sure that our voice is up to giving a speech, we always want to make sure that our efforts are going to count for something.

Speeches are not easy to give. We have to struggle with getting bad introductions, make sure that we offend a few people as possible if we are giving toasts, and be aware of all of the nonverbal signals that we are sending to our audience.

Because speaking can be so hard to so, when we get a chance to watch a famous person speak, we need to seize the opportunity – it's like going to speech giving school. They'll teach us critical skills like how to handle hecklers and how to give an effective keynote speech.

It may not always seem this way, but as speakers we do have power. We need to learn how to tap into the power that we have and use it to deliver the best speech that we possibly can.

For more information on what it takes to be a great public speaker, check out my blog, The Accidental Communicator, at:

www.TheAccidentalCommunicator.com

Good luck!

- Dr. Jim Anderson

About The Author

I must confess that I never set out to be a public speaker. When I went to school, I studied Computer Science and thought that I'd get a nice job programming and that would be that. Well, at least part of that plan worked out!

My first job was working for Boeing on their F/A-18 fighter jet program. I spent my days programming fighter jet software in assembly language and I loved it. The U.S. government decided to save some money and went looking for other countries to sell this plane to. This put me into an unfamiliar role: I started to meet with foreign military officials and I ended up having to give speeches in order to explain what my product did.

Time moved on and so did I. I found myself working for Siemens, the big German telecommunications company. They were making phone switches and selling them to the seven U.S. phone companies. The problem was that the switches were too complicated. Customers couldn't tell the difference between one complicated phone switch from another complicated phone switch. Once again I found myself standing in front of the room giving speeches in order to explain what these complicated machines did and why ours were better than anyone else's.

I've spent over 25 years working as a product manager for both big companies and startups. This has given me an opportunity to do many, many presentations for customers, at conferences, and everywhere in-between.

I now live in Tampa Florida where I spend my time managing my consulting business, Blue Elephant Consulting, teaching college courses at the University of South Florida, and traveling to work with companies like yours to share the knowledge that I have about how to create and deliver powerful and effective speeches.

I'm always available to answer questions and I can be reached at:

Dr. Jim Anderson
Blue Elephant Consulting
Email: jim@BlueElephantConsulting.com
Facebook: http://goo.gl/1TVoK
Web: **www.BlueElephantConsulting.com**

"Unforgettable communication skills that will set your ideas free…"

Create Speeches That Motivate Your Audiences And Get Your Message Heard!

Dr. Jim Anderson is available to provide training and coaching on the topics that are the most important to people who have to speak in public: how can I create a speech that people want to hear and how can I deliver in a way that will allow me to connect with my audience and get my point across to them?

Dr. Anderson believes that in order to both learn and remember what he says, speakers need to laugh. Each one of his speeches is full of fun and humor so that what he says "sticks" with everyone.

Dr. Anderson's Public Speaking Training Includes:

1. How to plan your next speech: pick your purpose and understand your audience.
2. What's the best way to get PowerPoint and Keynote to work with you, not against you?
3. What do you need to do when you are presenting in order to truly connect with your audience?

Dr. Jim Anderson presents over 100 speeches per year. To invite Dr. Anderson to speak at your event, contact him at: **Phone: 813-418-6970** or **Email: jim@BlueElephantConsulting.com**

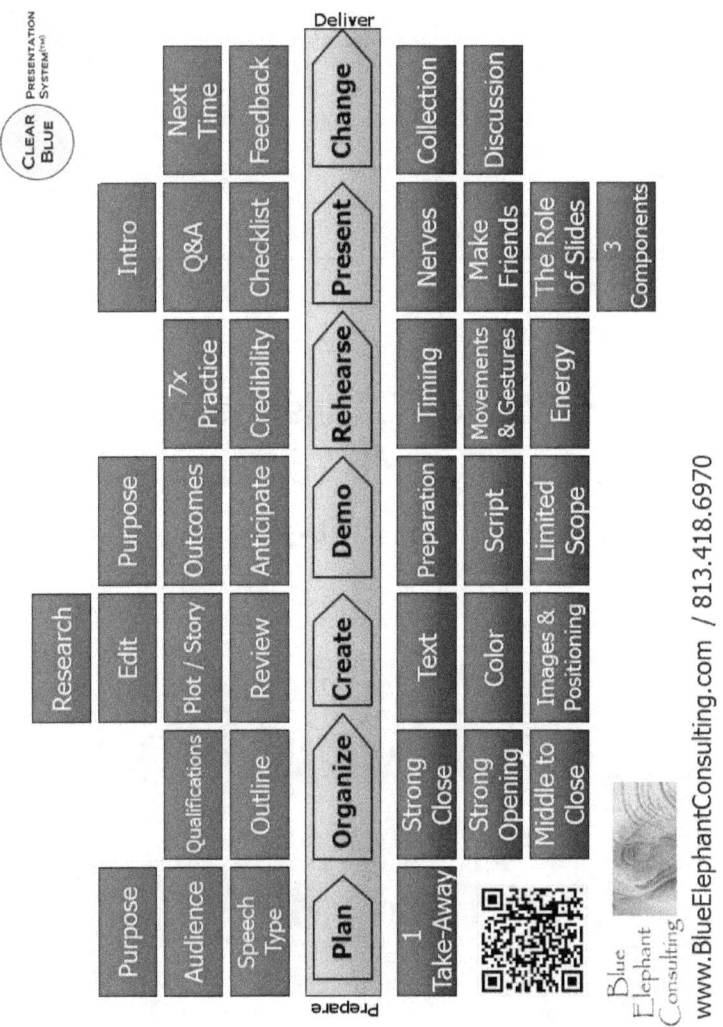

Blue Elephant Consulting has created the **Clear Blue™ Presentation System** for creating and delivering powerful and memorable presentations. The contents of this book are based on lessons learned during the development of the Clear Blue system. Contact Blue Elephant Consulting to learn more about the Clear Blue presentation system.

Chapter 1

Presentation Challenge: How To Successfully Talk To Teens – And Survive!

Chapter 1: Presentation Challenge: How To Successfully Talk To Teens – And Survive!

Anytime we speak in public it can be a challenge that gets our heart racing and causes us to start to sweat. However, if you really want to take the stress up a notch, then just try talking to a group of teens and watch your heart either start to beat double time or just stop altogether. Why do we have such a hang-up about presenting to teens?

I suspect it's because we don't quite know how best to talk to them: they are no longer kids, but they are not yet adults either. We simply don't feel that we know HOW to talk to them. Well get in line – I'm sure that their parents feel the same way! Let's have a talk with Pandora Scooter who for the past 15 years has been teaching and putting on workshops for teenagers all the time. She's got some tips that we can all use to get over ourselves and get on with the presentation...

Scooter points out that even the most experienced speakers seem to have a deep set fear of talking to a group of teenagers. When asked why they fear this audience more than a hall filled with over a 1,000 adults, they come back with answers such as "They won't care about what I have to say", "They won't listen to me", "I'm afraid of them". It turns out that just like with everything else in life, there is a grain of truth in what these speakers are saying.

Specifically, often teenagers will look like they aren't paying attention in order to appear "cool" to their friends – even though they may be hanging on your every word. If you can give them something to focus their attention on, then they will listen to you and you can make an impact. Here's what you need to do:

- **Challenge Them Right Off The Bat:** Your teen audience probably has been told to be there – they didn't decide to come by themselves. This means that they are expecting you to treat them just like every other adult does – assuming that they care about what you are going to be talking about. Turn this assumption on its head. Ask them a question, get them to raise their hands or stand up. Do SOMETHING to make sure that they realize that this is not just another boring presentation.

- **Stop Talking About Yourself:** In a nutshell, unless you are a rock star, your teen audience won't really care about where you've been or what awards you have won. Keep your introduction short and sweet – what's your name and why are you here?

- **Don't Be A Pushover:** If you take the time to be honest and direct with your teen audience, then they will respond. Almost without fail, there will other discussions that start up while you are talking or there will be people who are clearly not paying attention. You need to not ignore these events, but rather point them out and work out what is going on with the offenders. Simply by showing that you are paying attention to them and that you are not going to ignore them. This will catch their attention, and most of the time will solve the problem.

- **Say "Thank You":** By showing respect for your teen audience and expressing gratitude to them for their participation in your presentation you will capture their hearts and minds. This may seem like such a small thing, but saying "thank you" half-way through your presentation shows that you have something to base it on and warms the audience up for the rest of your presentation.

- **Use Your Eyes:** Eye contact can be the key to making your presentation a success. By making direct eye contact with members of your audience, you can ensure that they are engaged. You can take this one step further by calling out individual listeners and working them into your presentation "this gentlemen in black seems to be agreeing with me", etc. For an audience that is more used to being ignored, this will put them on their toes as they eagerly wait to see who get called out next.

- **Be Available:** At the end of a presentation to adults, you would probably tell them how they could get in contact with you if they needed any additional information. Make sure that you do the same thing for your teen audience. Hey, very few if any of the teens will actually take you up on your offer of further contact, but the simple fact that you made the offer will go a long way in gaining their respect and may make your message take hold at a deeper level.

Chapter 2

What To Do When You Say The Wrong Thing During A Presentation

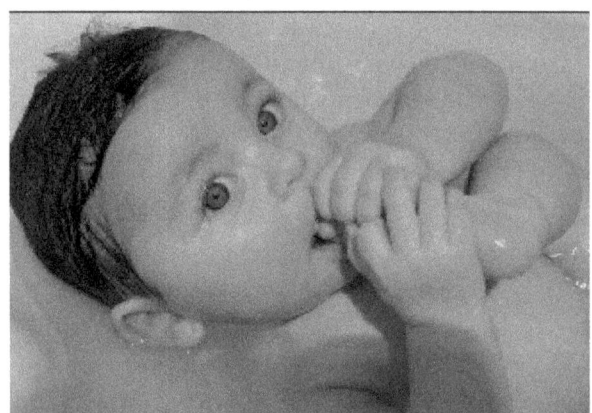

Chapter 2: What To Do When You Say The Wrong Thing During A Presentation

I'm sure that none of you would ever screw-up and make a verbal blunder during a presentation, right? There is an AT&T ad running right now that captures this concept – a guy has just told an office about an upcoming merger when he really was supposed to have not mentioned it (mayhem ensues). When giving a presentation, your best opportunity for a verbal blunder generally comes during the Q&A session. Here are some thoughts on how to cure yourself of foot-in-mouth disease…

During the recently concluded U.S. presidential race, both candidates were accomplished presenters. However, over and over again both sides said things that I'm sure they both really wished that they could take back. However, once said, your comments are what your audience will remember for better or for worse.

Experts at public speaking all agree on one thing: you can control what you say. Paul Sterman has done some research on this topic and has identified three things that you can do to prevent verbal blunders:

1. **Think Before You Speak:** It sounds like something your parents would tell you, but it really is that simple. We seem to get into the most trouble when we fire off our mouth without taking a moment to think about what we are going to say.

2. **Practice, Practice, Practice:** Even in a Q&A session, there is no reason for you to have not practiced responding to the questions that you knew were going to be asked. Remember: practice makes perfect.

3. **Get Some Sleep:** We end up saying the silliest things when we have not gotten enough sleep. Keep your mind sharp by making sure that you are well rested before giving any presentation.

When you are faced with a situation where you will be speaking extemporaneously, such as a Q&A session or when answering questions from employees, preparation is the key to not making a mistake that you might regret later on. Professional comedians are the ones who are best known for the practice that they put into making spur-of-the-moment statements seem to be not practiced. You want to be able to do the same.

Thinking through the questions that you might be asked and then creating a set of "talking points" that you would use to respond to such questions is the key to preventing a verbal stumble. Your goal is to create "sound bites" that people will remember just like politicians do.

Finally, although it may seem like you need to reply immediately when someone asks you a question during a presentation, there is no rule that says that you have to. You are in charge of how and when you respond to each question asked. Take a moment, think about what the person is really asking, and then provide them with an appropriate answer.

Of course the old saying that the more you do something, the better you get at it is also true here. Instead of fearing speaking opportunities where you might stumble over your words, instead view it as a learning opportunity that will make you stronger for the times that you really need to be at your best.

Chapter 3

How To Prepare Your Voice For Your Next Presentation

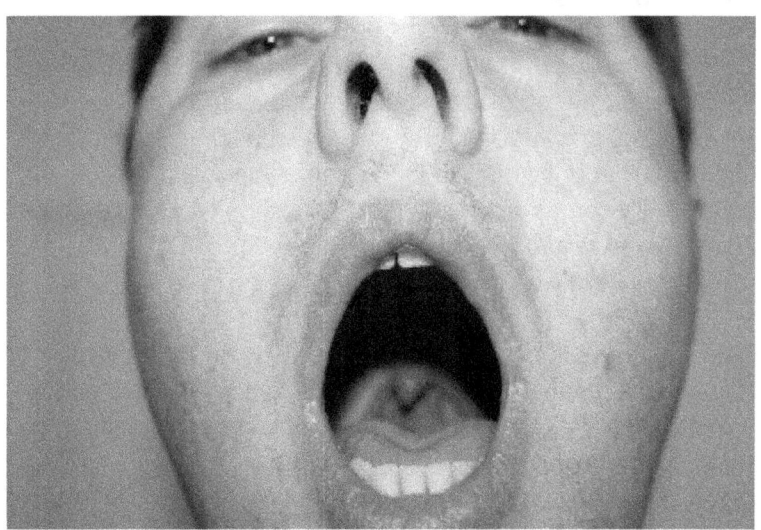

Chapter 3: How To Prepare Your Voice For Your Next Presentation

We can spend all the time in the world talking about how to prepare better presentations, capture and hold your audience's attention, create great PowerPoint slides, etc. and it will all be for naught if we forget to talk about one very important thing: your voice. I don't know about you guys, but I really don't spend very much time thinking about my voice – until it's not there!

So if everything is going along fine, then you don't really need to worry about your voice. However, if you have a big presentation coming up, that's when things can start to get bad in a hurry. You pick the cause: weather changes, allergies, a cold or flu, no matter the cause – the results are always the same. If there is something wrong with your voice, then that's what your audience is going to be focusing on – not what you are saying!

We all have ways of dealing with sore body parts that we can get to like an arm or a leg. How does one go about taking care of a voice that is located "in there" somewhere? It turns out that it really comes down to a list of things that you SHOULD be doing as well as another list of things that you SHOULD NOT be doing. Let's take a look…

Fluids, fluids, fluids. In the end, having a healthy / happy voice requires that you keep your vocal cords supple. Ways to do this include drinking fluids such as sports drinks which replenish sugars, sodium and lots of other nutrients.

Of course, there is a flip side to this – you need to stop drinking some things. You can say goodbye to coffee as your presentation date / time grows nearer. Oh, the same thing goes for alcohol in any form. The reason that you have to avoid these fluids is because they act as a drying agent and that's the last thing that your vocal cords need.

How do you start your day? I personally enjoy having a glass of orange juice. However, it turns out that orange juice has the potential to irritate your throat. Dang! The OJ has to go on presentation day.

If you start to come down with something as your big presentation day approaches, there are some defensive activities that you can start to do. Adding a humidifier to your bedroom will help to lubricate your throat while you are sleeping. Additionally, you can spend some time in a steamy shower in order to sooth your entire respiratory system.

Once you get your fluids taken care of, you need to make sure that you don't screw things up now. This means that you need to avoid clearing your throat because this will end up irritating your vocal cords.

If you feel yourself starting to become hoarse there are a couple of things that you can do. Try to gargle with warm salt water a few times during the day. Additionally, you should start to drink herbal tea with honey in order to fight back the hoarseness.

Be very careful about doing what we all normally do: popping a throat lozenges that contains menthol or some other anesthetics. The reason that these are so bad for you is that they numb your throat and this will hide your body's warning signs that it's time to stop using your voice.

One final recommendation: during your actual presentation you should do your best to keep your tone at a conversational volume level. By doing this you will be able to avoid overexerting your vocal cords.

Chapter 4

I Hear Your Body Talking...

Chapter 4: It's All About The Nonverbal, Presenter

So we stand up, walk to the front of the room, and start our presentation. All too often, we seem to think that we are the only conversation going on in the room at any given time. It turns out that we're wrong – there's a whole lot of nonverbal stuff going on between us and our audience. Maybe we should take a look at what we are saying…

Dr. Alex "Sandy" Pentland is a researcher who works at MIT's Media Lab. He's been working on trying to use technology to capture the nonverbal signals that we are giving off so that we can better understand what we are "saying". He's a recognized expert in this field and is the author of a new book called Honest Signals: How They Shape Our World

Dr. Pentland's approach to answering these questions has been to invent something that he calls a "sociometer". This is a wearable badge-like device that uses technology to constantly measure all sorts of nonverbal aspects of how people communicate.

What Dr. Pentland has discovered is valuable stuff for us presenters. One discovery that he's made is that you can measure how interested people are in something by measuring the timing between two people who are having a conversation. If they are anticipating when the other one will pause and then jumping in right then and leaving no gaps in the conversation, then you know that they are paying a lot of attention to each other.

From a presenter's point-of-view, since we are really having a one-way conversation with our audience, we need to create this anticipation. You need to be having a dialog with your audience and you need to be asking them a lot of questions. As they anticipate your questions and mentally prepare answers, they will become more and more engaged in what you are saying.

Dr. Pentland has also been able to measure that part of us that "mirrors" another person. When we watch someone move, the part of our brain that corresponds to that action fires up – this is called mirroring. When we mimic each other's gestures during a conversation, this causes feelings of trust and empathy to occur.

As a presenter we can use this knowledge in two different ways. First, by moving around during our presentations we can keep our audience more mentally awake because their brains will constantly be firing trying to mirror our actions. Secondly, if when we are making a key point we take the time to physically mirror our audience (stop moving, stand straight up, hands at our sides), they will accept what we have to say more readily.

Dr. Pentland's last area of observation has been in fluency or consistency. The best example of this these days is Tiger Wood's golf swing – smooth and fluid. It turns out that when you are consistent in your tone or your motions, then this tells your audience that you really know what you're doing (or at least have really practiced it!)

For a presenter, this means that we really do have to practice our speeches before we give them. Every time we practice saying the words, we become just a little bit more fluid and just a bit smoother.

Finally, Dr. Pentland took some time and studied people who were presenting business cases in order to get funding. What he found is that it really didn't matter WHAT they said, the same ones would always get funded. These were the ones who were the most excited about their plans.

The final note for us presenters is that we ALWAYS have to find a way to get excited about what we are presenting. We may not realize it, but our excitement level is a key nonverbal message that comes through loud and clear every time we present.

Chapter 5

How Presenters Can Give A Toast Without Toasting A Relationship

Chapter 5: How Presenters Can Give A Toast Without Toasting A Relationship

So you've been invited to a wedding, a retirement party, or some other celebration in which friends and family are going to gather in order to honor someone. There will probably be some sort of food served, drinks will flow, and then someone will do it – they'll stand up and give a toast. Oh, oh – now it's your turn to do the same thing. How are you going to do this without looking like a fool or destroying your relationship with the person(s) of honor?

First off, get rid of any plans that you might have to say something naughty. Rarely will this go over well; however, more often than not it falls flat on its face and so just say "no". Michael Varma is a professional speaker who has seen his fair share of toasting disasters and he's got some advice for all of us.

Michael says that when you are giving a toast, you should always start out by introducing yourself – in a crowd of people, there are probably a bunch of folks who don't know who you are. Also spell out how you are related to the person(s) of honor because this will help to make your toast clearer. Michael suggests that your actual toast have three characteristics: make it brief, make it bold, and then be done with it.

A toast is NOT a speech! Mark Twain probably said it best when he recommended that toasts should never be longer than 1 minute. The longer your toast, the less impact that it will have. The "air time" that you are taking for your toast belongs to everyone and you need to use as little of it as possible.

When you are giving a toast, this is not the time to be shy. You are probably talking to a noisy room in which people may be eating, drinking, and having their own side conversations. You need to speak up! Your goal should be to speak loudly enough that everyone in the room, including the folks in the back, can hear you clearly.

When you are done speaking, shut up and sit down. Yes you've just given a performance; however, this event is not all about you so don't do any bowing or waving. Shut your mouth and sit down so that everyone can once again return their attention to the person(s) of honor.

If you want your toast to be memorable, then the trick is to tell a story. I must once again reemphasize a key point – keep it clean! Don't tell stories about old girlfriends at a wedding and don't tell stories about stealing office supplies at a retirement party. Instead, tell a story that shows the person(s) of honor in a good light. Oh, and keep it to under a minute.

I have always found wedding toasts to be a bit of a challenge. There are too many ways that things can go wrong, too many people that you could end up offending. Over the course of time, I have refined and polished my wedding toast so that it goes something like this:

"Friends and family, we are gathered here to celebrate the wedding of ... They are who they are because the people in this room have taken the time to shape and mold them into the people that they have become today – and for that we apologize! However, from this day forward, it will be up to them to determine together who they want to become and we wish them all the luck in doing so."

So there you go, a little sappy, a little funny, and hopefully just right for a toast.

Chapter 6

D.O.A.: Why Presenters Hate Bad Introductions

Chapter 6: D.O.A.: Why Presenters Hate Bad Introductions

We spend all of this time coming up with our next speech, getting each and every word just right, practicing the speech, the gestures, and the pauses, only **to get killed** before we even open our mouths to speak.

How does this crime occur? Simple – whoever is running the show delivers a **bad introduction** and then turns the stage over to us. Just imagine the total silence that grips the room then – all of a sudden there is no excitement about who you are or what you are going to be saying. Talk about having to dig yourself out of a hole before you even start!

Michael Varma is a professional speaker who had found himself in this situation a number of times and has come up with some ways **to avoid it**.

First off, as a presenter you've got to spend some time thinking about just **what an introduction is designed to do**. In the world of professional comedy, a warm-up act comes out before the main act. The role of the warm-up act is simply to get the audience used to laughing. This makes things much easier for the main act – the audience is already conditioned to laugh no matter what the main act says. An introduction does the same thing for a presenter.

As a presenter, you need to come up with a good introduction for yourself and your speech. A good introduction needs to contain **three things**:

- **Content**: What are you going to be talking about? This is designed to grab your audience's attention so that they will be eager to hear more.

- **Context**: Just knowing WHAT you will be talking about is not enough, your audience needs to know WHY you will be talking about it and why they should care. Providing them with this information will start to build a bridge between you on stage and the audience even before you start to speak.

- **Credibility**: Providing the audience with a reason why you are the best person to be talking to them about this topic is the final part of an introduction. All too often we put too much information here (we are, after all, proud of ourselves). In all honesty, one or two sentences does the trick.

Look, you can't always control the way life goes and sometimes you will be introduced poorly. However, if you write out your introduction, print it out nice and large and provide it to your introducer BEFORE he or she goes on stage, then you will have done your best to **avoid being a victim** of the crime of a poor introduction.

Chapter 7

Real Life Speeches: George Halvorson, CEO Of Kaiser Foundation Health Plan, Inc.

Chapter 7: Real Life Speeches: George Halvorson, CEO Of Kaiser Foundation Health Plan, Inc.

We can talk about how to be a better communicator all we want, but in the end it comes down to learning – and we all do this in different ways. One great way to discover what a speaker should (or should not) do is to watch 'em in action. This time around we're going to take a look at how a powerful CEO, George Halvorson, did during a recent **keynote speech**.

Halvorson is the Chairman and CEO of the Kaiser Permanente health system. There's no question that he knows his stuff, the challenge will be to discover **how well he can communicate it**.

While attending the recent HIMSS health care show up in Chicago, I had an opportunity to watch Halvorson in action as he gave a keynote speech. How did he do? Overall – **not bad**, but it could have been better. Let's find out how.

- **Nerves:** First off, this was a big presentation. In the audience were approximately 10,000 – 12,000 eager listeners. We all talk about getting butterflies in our guts before we talk, but just image how Halvorson must have felt?

- **Introduction:** That being said, the lead in to Halvorson's speech was spectacular. A professionally produced video and well done sound track listed all of his accomplishments. It was rock show quality stuff and everyone was pumped up and ready for a good speech by the time he took the podium.

- **Opening:** That's when the ball got dropped. The first words out of your mouth have to be grabbers – they have to convince your audience to pay attention to what you are going to be saying. Halvorson's were, unfortunately, forgettable. He started by thanking people and commenting on the convention – pleasant talk that went nowhere.

- **Humor:** It turns out that Halvorson has a great sense of humor. Although this was a high-stakes keynote speech, he was able to work his humor into it and this really allowed him to connect with his audience. He came across not as an aloof CEO, but rather as a real guy who is trying to solve problems.

- **Notes:** Reading from your notes is always a bad idea. Halvorson did a lot of this and it showed. Now I'll grant that this was a big speech and there were multimedia issues – he had to synch up with the folks who were controlling the slide show. Still, when you read your speech word-for-word you lose that connection with your audience.

- **Hands:** what to do with your hands during a speech is always a big question. Halvorson did pretty well, but he still struggled at times. As we all have a tendency to do, he put his hands on the podium and even leaned on it at times. When he made gestures with his hands, they were down low and couldn't be seen by the people in the back of the room. However, there was one point in time in which his right hand was used in a hammering gesture that drove home the point that he was making.

We can practice our public speaking by ourselves as much as we want, but having the opportunity to **watch and learn from others** is, as the folks at Visa tell us, priceless.

Chapter 8

Real Life Speeches: Alan Greenspan Gives A Keynote

Chapter 8: Real Life Speeches: Alan Greenspan Gives A Keynote

Even if you don't work in the world of high-finance, you surely know who Alan Greenspan is. He was the chairman of the U.S. Federal Reserve from 1987 to 2006. There's no question that this guy is smart, but can he deliver a **good keynote speech**?

Where It Happened

While attending the recent HIMSS health care show up in Chicago, I had an opportunity to watch Greenspan in action as he gave a keynote speech. Now you have to understand that he was speaking on the third day of a 3-day conference and generally the crowds would have thinned out by now, but that wasn't the case. The hall in which he gave his speech had a seating capacity of 15,000 – 20,000 and it was **pretty much full**.

What caught my interest was that people were not showing up because they thought that Greenspan was a good speaker. No, they were showing up because they wanted to **hear the information** that they thought that he would be communicating: how did the current recession come about and when will it end?

The Introduction

The lead up to Greenspan's keynote speech was a spectacular Hollywood introduction. Lights flashed, the speakers boomed with an announcer's voice, and a brief film played that showed all of Greenspan's many accomplishments. This was followed up by the Chairman of the HIMSS organization coming on stage and reading a prepared introduction for Greenspan. **What speaker could ask for a better intro?**

The Speech

So I know that the question that you are dying to have answered is "how did he do?" The answer is that Alan Greenspan **is not a very good keynote speaker**; however, the audience hung on his every word. Perhaps some explanation is needed here:

- **Technical Knowledge:** Greenspan knows his stuff. He was there to explain how the U.S. economy works and the introduction plus the words that came out of his mouth confirmed that he really knows his stuff.

- **Hands**: Greenspan's #1 problem with public speaking is that he, just like so many other speakers, has no idea what to do with his hands. During his keynote speech his hands spent the time traveling from his pants pockets to being clasped and back again. It was a big room and only his face was displayed on the jumbo-tron screens, but it was distracting none the less.

- **Technical Content:** I'm not sure what the rest of the audience was expecting, but I was anticipating a watered-down speech on basic economics. I was flat out wrong. Greenspan held no punches back and used very technical economic terms in his speech about how the world's economy operates.

- **Pacing:** The stage that Greenspan was giving his keynote speech on was HUGE. He was equipped with a wireless mic and so he could go anywhere. Unfortunately, he did. He paced back and forth and moved from side to side. Now there is no problem doing this if it supports your speech, but there was no clear linkage between his movements and his speech.

- **Using Notes:** The first 25% of Greenspan's keynote was delivered pretty much how you would expect a keynote to be delivered – he had some notes that he referred to occasionally, but the rest of the time he looked at the audience and spoke. However, just a little bit of the way into his speech, something strange happened – he picked up his notes and started reading from them word-for-word. The impact of his speech went way down when it felt like he was reading a book to us.

What Was Learned From All Of This

I had been very excited to listen to Greenspan speak – he is basically a rock-star in the world of finance. I came away from his keynote speech feeling just a little bit let down. On one hand, I was amazed at just **how powerful a reputation can be** in drawing people to come to a speech just to hear what the speaker has to say. Substance over style so to speak.

On the other hand, the reading word-for-word from notes really disappointed me. Then an interesting thing happened, I think that I figured out why he did it. Greenspan seemed to be a perfectly competent speaker. I don't think that he NEEDED to read his speech from his notes. However, I now think that **he is such an important person** that the words that come out of his mouth can still move markets.

This means that, just like the President of the Unites States, he has to be very careful about what he says (and how he says it). If he had said that "… the recession is going to last for another 5 years…" then the stock market would have plunged the next day. Perhaps reading his speech was **a way to protect us all** from words that are too powerful…!

Chapter 9

Dennis Quaid Gives A Keynote Speech
– Real Life Speeches

Chapter 9: Dennis Quaid Gives A Keynote Speech – Real Life Speeches

I just got back from spending the better part of a week up in Chicago at a big health care conference (HIMSS09). This was an amazing opportunity for me to sit back and watch somewhere in the neighborhood of about 100 different presenters get up and do their very best job at communicating. One of these presenters was Dennis Quaid – the actor.

What was Dennis Quaid doing at a fairly boring health care IT conference you ask? Well it turns out that he has a heck of a story to tell about how his newborn children were given the wrong medicine. Everyone attending the conference knew about the story, and so roughly 15,000 – 20,000 folks showed up to hear Dennis give his speech.

So how did it go? Well, in all honesty, not that well. I mean, it was ok – but not what everyone was really hoping for. Generally when you show up for a keynote speech, you are expecting a great speech. When the speaker is a famous actor, your expectations are that much higher. Things didn't start as well as you would have hoped that they would have.

Dennis was introduced by a slick video that reminded the audience of all of the movies that he has been in. He then came out and took control of the podium. This is where things started to fall apart. His first few statements dealt with how he's not really a doctor and how he really has never played a role in the health care industry. These are all true things, but what a lousy way to start a speech to folks who ARE in the health care industry!

Add to this a great deal of hemming and hawing, playing with his hands, and just all around nervousness and you end up with a speaker who is distracting his audience away from what is a very powerful message. So what was going on here?

I'll never know the exact answer, but here are a few guesses. Dennis Quaid is an actor. He sure seems to do a great job of performing for a camera – in front a film crew of about 40 people or so. Put him in front of 20,000 folks sitting in chairs in a massive convention hall and he may feel the same way that any one of us would feel – incredibly nervous.

One other contributing factor may have been that the story that he was there to tell was a VERY personal story. It's entirely possible that each time he tells it, the emotions that the story stirs up in him causes him to fall apart.

No matter what the cause, the effect was the same – a less than expected speech. Us mere mortals can learn much from Dennis Quaid's challenges. First, practice, practice, practice – no matter how good you think you are, everyone is going to be able to tell if you try to "wing it". Secondly, practice in front of people that you know – their feedback can tell you things that you can't see yourself.

Chapter 10

Can You Hear Me Now Is What Presenters Need To Know

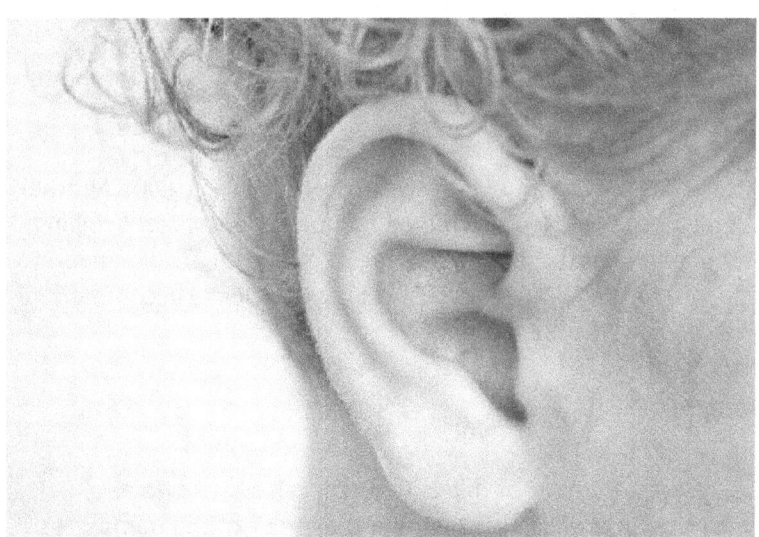

Chapter 10: Can You Hear Me Now Is What Presenters Need To Know

When we are given an opportunity to address a group, we spend a great deal of time preparing what we are going to say and how we are going to say it. This is all well and good, but we may be forgetting one critical factor: our audience may not be able to hear us speak.

Why Can't They Hear Us?

Even if you have the most interesting story to tell your audience, they may not be able to hear you tell it. Rick Moore is a professional freelance writer who speaks in public and he knows a great deal about this because he has a hearing loss and this has caused him to study audiences. He points out that in the U.S. there are 26 million people who have permanent hearing damage. What are the odds that one or more of them will be in your next audience?

Rick notes that as though this wasn't enough, there are another 12 million people who suffer from tinnitus – a constant ringing in the ears. Put these numbers together and clearly you need to change the way you've been speaking in order to accommodate this portion of your audience.

Things To Do So That A Speaker Can Be Heard

There are a number of things that you can start to do as a presenter in order to better meet the needs of the members of your audience who have hearing problems. These include:

- **Room Awareness**: We are probably already aware of the lighting and the microphone setup – now we need to become aware of the acoustics. The key here is to pick a spot to stand at that you will be able to be easily heard from everywhere in the room.

- **Speak Up!**: This one is pretty obvious, but it's an important point – in order to be heard by your audience you are going to have to project your voice. Quiet whispering won't cut it – make sure that you are speaking to be heard in the back of the room.

- **Practice Age Discrimination**: No, not the bad kind – the good kind. Take a look at your audience – what does their average age appear to be? The older the audience, the greater the possibility that some members will have hearing problems. This means that you need to be extra vigilant in keeping your volume up and using very clear diction.

- **Show 'Em Your Lips**: Even if your audience members don't read lips, looking out at them so that they can see your lips moving while you speak, instead of down at your notes, will give them another visual clue that will help them decode what you are saying.

Final Thoughts

These tips are a great way to address the general hearing needs of your next audience. However, as you are giving your next speech you may discover that someone in your audience appears to be becoming bored or disinterested. It could be because despite your best efforts they can't hear you.

The correct thing to do in this circumstance is to adapt to the situation. Move close to where they are sitting, look directly at them more often, and use more pauses so that they can more easily interpret your words.

Making sure that everyone can hear you helps you to better accomplish your goal in giving the presentation: changing lives for the better.

Chapter 11

Handling Hecklers: 5 Ways That Presenters Can Restore Order

Chapter 11: Handling Hecklers: 5 Ways That Presenters Can Restore Order

How does that children's rhyme go?

"Sticks and stones will break my bones, but words will never hurt me".

Bull! If there is one thing that presenters dread more than forgetting their lines, it's having someone add to their speech without an invitation. Unlike President Obama we don't have a flock of **Secret Service agents** at our beck and call who can fan out into an audience and cart off an unruly heckler.

What should you do when someone in the audience starts to deliberately take away from your carefully rehearsed speech? Start crying and go home is always a possibility; however, I've got some **better ways** to deal with this situation for you...

What Is Heckling?

Maybe a good place for us to start this discussion is to make sure that we both fully understand just what **heckling** is. There are two types of heckling that you **WILL** have to deal with during one or more of your presentations: active and passive.

Active heckling occurs when someone in the audience starts talking back to you right in the middle of your speech. For a public speaker this often feels like you've just hit a speed bump in your speech while you were going 80 miles an hour. Talk about surprising!

Passive heckling is much closer to disrespect. This often shows up as people having their own conversations during your presentation. Normally this is their own call and you don't really care, but if they are loud enough then it becomes your problem.

Talking on a cell phone or having a huddle at the back of the room are common ways that this shows up.

No matter if you are speaking at a wedding, a graduation, or a business function, hecklers will **ALWAYS** be in the audience and it's just a matter if they decide to speak up. First off, we should talk about what you should **NOT** do...

What Should You NOT Do?

I sorta like to think of this as the North Korea problem – man they are annoying, but they are so small as to not really count in the big scheme of things. Likewise, when you are faced with either an active or a passive heckler, you need to make sure that you don't come out with **guns 'a blazing**. Here are a few things that you should **NOT** do when you are trying to deal with a heckler:

- **Don't try to be funny**: this is the #1 response that trips up most presenters. They spend too much time trying to come up with a funny response to the heckler on the spot and it falls flat. A serious response will shut him/her up most of the time.

- **Don't Lose Your Temper**: I don't care if you were just coming to that point in your speech which causes everyone to burst into tears and now this rude heckler has spoiled the moment. If you lose your temper, then you'll never be able to get back into your speech after the moment has passed.

How To Correctly Handle A Heckler

Some hecklers are a one-shot deal – they make one comment and then they'll go away forever. However, depending on what they've said, even this type of heckler needs to be dealt with.

Dealing with all types of hecklers correctly is the key to being a successful public speaker. Here are **5 ways** that you can deal with hecklers during your speech:

1. **Silence**: Somewhat surprisingly the simplest solution is often the most effective. If you stop speaking and turn and stare at the heckler, everyone else will turn to see what you are looking at. In 95% of heckler cases this kind of social embarrassment is all that it takes to shut a heckler up.

2. **Tie Your Response To The Event**: This is a clever way to remind the heckler why everyone is at the event. For example, if you were speaking at a breast cancer awareness event and started to have problems with a heckler, a great response would be "Hey, I'm talking here – unless you've discovered a way to beat breast cancer, how about if you just remain quiet".

3. **Add The Heckler To Your Team**: This technique turns an unexpected interruption into what appears to be a planned part of your speech. After the heckler has said what they are going to say, pause for a moment and thank your "speechwriter / joke writer / etc.". The audience will laugh with you, the heckler will beam with pride, and you can go on.

4. **Give Them The Mic**: This is a fairly drastic tactic, but it can pay great dividends. Walk over to where the heckler is sitting and offer to hand them the mic. Generally they will decline the offer and will get the point that this presentation is not all about them.

5. **Think Outside The Room**: Certain hecklers, such as loud groups at the back of the room, can resist all efforts on your part to overcome them. This calls for innovative thinking. One way to handle this is either for you or

your audience to move. You can move out into the center of your audience and deliver your speech "in the round" or you can have them move their chairs in order to be closer to you.

Final Thoughts

When I'm starting a speech, I always try to keep in mind that there are **two groups in the room** – me and everyone else. A heckler poses a unique problem in that if not dealt with correctly, he/she can drive a wedge in between me and my audience.

Ultimately what a great speaker tries to do is to separate the heckler from the rest of the audience so that there are **three groups in the room**: you, the audience, and the heckler. If you can accomplish this, then you'll be able to silence the heckler while at the same time intimately connecting with your audience and make a lasting impact in their lives.

Chapter 12

Speaking Power: How To Get It, How To Use It

Chapter 12: Speaking Power: How To Get It, How To Use It

If you really want to connect with your audience and make an impact in their lives, then you're going to have to discover hot how to **speak with power**. The trick is that power is a tricky thing – you can't touch it, you can't buy it, you've got to find it and hold on to it. The good news is that I know how you can do this...

It Isn't All About The Slides

In the quest for speaking power, all too often speakers attempt to create the very best **PowerPoint slides** in the vain hope that if they have powerful slides, then their speech will also have power. Sorry, it doesn't work this way.

George Torok is a professional speaker who has spent time studying how speakers use PowerPoint slides. He's come up with the three following observations:

1. **Everybody Uses PowerPoint**: one of the big problems with PowerPoint is that everyone uses it – it's not special. No matter how good your slides are, your audience has seen similar slides like that before.

2. **PowerPoint Is Easy To Use**: because it's easy to use, it's all too easy to start to believe that your slides are the centerpiece of your presentation. This is not the case and many presenters have been fooled.

3. **Good Slides Can Cover A Bad Presenter**: the belief that fantastic slides can smooth over flaws in a presentation has lead too many speakers to fall flat during their presentations.

Where Does Power Really Come From?

It turns out that the power that you need in order to deliver an effective presentation comes **from within you**. If you believe in yourself and the message that you are delivering, then you'll have the power that you need to give an effective presentation. Once you believe in yourself, your next job is to convey power to your audience.

Projecting Power

In order to communicate your power to your audience, you'll need to do the following four things:

1. **Look Powerful**: How you physically look to your audience is the first step in communicating your power to your audience. The simplest way to do this is to smile at your audience. This helps you to convey both trust and confidence.

2. **Posture Counts**: Taking the time to stand up straight. All too often we stoop over and hunch our shoulders as we focus on what we are saying. If we stand up straight we'll be projecting power to our audience.

3. **Use Your Voice**: One of a speaker's most powerful tools is your voice. In order to communicate power to your audience, you need to speak slowly and deepen your voice. Additionally, using pauses and actually saying less will allow more time for your words to sink in with your audience.

4. **Your Words Count**: keeping your words short and simple will allow your speech to have more power than using longer more complicated words. The harder it is

for your audience to understand and comprehend your message, the more diluted your power will be.

It's from the forge of failure that the steel of success is formed.

Hard Work Does Not Guarantee Success, But Success Does Not Happen Without Hard Work.

- Dr. Jim Anderson

Create Speeches That Motivate Your Audiences And Get Your Message Heard!

Dr. Jim Anderson is available to provide training and coaching on the topics that are the most important to people who have to speak in public: how can I create a speech that people want to hear and how can I deliver in a way that will allow me to connect with my audience and get my point across to them?

Dr. Anderson believes that in order to both learn and remember what he says, speakers need to laugh. Each one of his speeches is full of fun and humor so that what he says "sticks" with everyone.

Dr. Anderson's Public Speaking Training Includes:

1. How to plan your next speech: pick your purpose and understand your audience.
2. What's the best way to get PowerPoint and Keynote to work with you, not against you?
3. What do you need to do when you are presenting in order to truly connect with your audience?

Dr. Jim Anderson presents over 100 speeches per year. To invite Dr. Anderson to speak at your event, contact him at: **Phone: 813-418-6970** or **Email: jim@BlueElephantConsulting.com**

Photo Credits:

Cover – ImagineCup
https://www.flickr.com/photos/imaginecup/

Chapter 1 - By: Casa Thomas Jefferson
https://www.flickr.com/photos/ctjonline/

Chapter 2 – bradleyolin
https://www.flickr.com/photos/yarhargoat/

Chapter 3 - Jeff and Mandy G
https://www.flickr.com/photos/mandyandjeffg/

Chapter 4 - Eric E Castro
https://www.flickr.com/photos/ecastro/2469265063/

Chapter 5 - Matt DeTurck
https://www.flickr.com/photos/dalboz17/

Chapter 6 - Vector Open Stock
https://www.flickr.com/photos/freevectorstock/

Chapter 7 - Robert Scoble
https://www.flickr.com/photos/scobleizer/

Chapter 8 - The Aspen Institute
https://www.flickr.com/photos/aspeninstitute/

Chapter 9 – allenmock
https://www.flickr.com/photos/susanandallen/

Chapter 10 - Shai Barzilay
https://www.flickr.com/photos/shyb/

Chapter 11 - Allan Rostron
https://www.flickr.com/photos/arostron/6857818591/

Chapter 12 – SparkCBC
https://www.flickr.com/photos/25031050@N06/

Other Books By The Author

Product Management

- How To Create A Successful Product That Customers Will Want: Techniques For Product Managers To Boost Product Sales And Increase Customer Satisfaction

- What Product Managers Need To Know About World-Class Product Development: How Product Managers Can Create Successful Products

- How Product Managers Can Learn To Understand Their Customers: Techniques For Product Managers To Better Understand What Their Customers Really Want

- Product Management Secrets: Techniques For Product Managers To Boost Product Sales And Increase Customer Satisfaction

- Product Development Lessons For Product Managers: How Product Managers Can Create Successful Products

- Customer Lessons For Product Managers: Techniques For Product Managers To Better Understand What Their Customers Really Want

- Product Failure Lessons For Product Managers: Examples Of Products That Have Failed For Product Managers To Learn From

- Communication Skills For Product Managers: The Communication Skills That Product Managers Need To Know How To Use In Order To Have A Successful Product

- How To Have A Successful Product Manager Career: The Things That You Need To Be Doing TODAY In Order To Have A Successful Product Manager Career

- Product Manager Product Success: How to keep your product on track and make it become a success

Public Speaking

- Tools Speakers Need In Order To Give The Perfect Speech: What tools to use to create your next speech so that your message will be remembered forever!

- How To Create A Speech That Will Be Remembered

- Secrets To Organizing A Speech For Maximum Impact: How to put together a speech that will capture and hold your audience's attention

- How To Become A Better Speaker By Changing How You Speak: Change techniques that will transform a speech into a memorable event

- How To Give A Great Presentation: Presentation techniques that will transform a speech into a memorable event

- How To Rehearse In Order To Give The Perfect Speech: How to effectively rehearse your next speech to that your message be remembered forever!

- Secrets To Creating The Perfect Speech: How to create a speech that will make your message be remembered forever!

- Secrets To Organizing The Perfect Speech: How to organize the best speech of your life!

- Secrets To Planning The Perfect Speech: How to plan to give the best speech of your life

- How To Show What You Mean During A Presentation: How to use visual techniques to transform a speech into a memorable event

CIO Skills

- Becoming A Powerful And Effective Leader: Tips And Techniques That IT Managers Can Use In Order To Develop Leadership Skills

- CIO Secrets For Growing Innovation: Tips And Techniques For CIOs To Use In Order To Make Innovation Happen In Their IT Department

- Your Success As A CIO Depends On How Well You Communicate: Tips And Techniques For CIOs To Use In Order To Become Better Communicators

- What CIOs Need To Know About Working With Partners: Techniques For CIOs To Use In Order To Be Able To Successfully Work With Partners

- Critical CIO Management Skills: Decision Making Skills That Every CIO Needs To Have In Order To Be Able To Make The Right Choices

- How CIOs Can Make Innovation Happen: Tips And Techniques For CIOs To Use In Order To Make

Innovation Happen In Their IT Department

- CIO Communication Skills Secrets: Tips And Techniques For CIOs To Use In Order To Become Better Communicators

- Managing Your CIO Career: Steps That CIOs Have To Take In Order To Have A Long And Successful Career

- CIO Business Skills: How CIOs can work effectively with the rest of the company!

IT Manager Skills

- Save Yourself, Save Your Job – How To Manage Your IT Career: Secrets That IT Managers Can Use In Order To Have A Successful Career

- Growing Your CIO Career: How CIOs Can Work With The Entire Company In Order To Be Successful

- How IT Managers Can Make Innovation Happen: Tips And Techniques For IT Managers To Use In Order To Make Innovation Happen In Their Teams

- Staffing Skills IT Managers Must Have: Tips And Techniques That IT Managers Can Use In Order To

Correctly Staff Their Teams

- Secrets Of Effective Leadership For IT Managers: Tips And Techniques That IT Managers Can Use In Order To Develop Leadership Skills

- IT Manager Career Secrets: Tips And Techniques That IT Managers Can Use In Order To Have A Successful Career

- IT Manager Budgeting Skills: How IT Managers Can Request, Manage, Use, And Track Their Funding

- Secrets Of Managing Budgets: What IT Managers Need To Know In Order To Understand How Their Company Uses Money

Negotiating

- Learn How To Signal In Your Next Negotiation: How To Develop The Skill Of Effective Signaling In A Negotiation In Order To Get The Best Possible Outcome

- Learn The Skill Of Exploring In A Negotiation: How To Develop The Skill Of Exploring What Is Possible In A Negotiation In Order To Reach The Best Possible Deal

- Learn How To Argue In Your Next Negotiation: How To Develop The Skill Of Effective Arguing In A Negotiation In Order To Get The Best Possible Outcome|

- How To Open Your Next Negotiation: How To Start A Negotiation In Order To Get The Best Possible Outcome

- Preparing For Your Next Negotiation: What You Need To Do BEFORE A Negotiation Starts In Order To Get The Best Possible Deal

- Learn How To Package Trades In Your Next Negotiation

- All Good Things Come To An End: How To Close A Negotiation - How To Develop The Skill Of Closing In Order To Get The Best Possible Outcome From A Negotiation

- Take No Prisoners In Your Next Negotiation: How To Start A Negotiation In Order To Get The Best Possible Outcome

Miscellaneous

- The Internet-Enabled Successful School District Superintendent: How To Use The Internet To Boost Parental Involvement In Your Schools

- Power Distribution Unit (PDU) Secrets: What Everyone Who Works In A Data Center Needs To Know!

- Making The Jump: How To Land Your Dream Job When You Get Out Of College!

- How To Use The Internet To Create Successful Students And Involved Parents

"Presentation techniques that will transform a speech into a memorable event"

This book has been written with one goal in mind – to show you how you can present a powerful and effective speech. We're going to show you how to use the tools that every speaker has to deliver a great speech!

Let's Make Your Next Speech A Success!

What You'll Find Inside:

- **PRESENTATION CHALLENGE: HOW TO SUCCESSFULLY TALK TO TEENS – AND SURVIVE!**

- **WHAT TO DO WHEN YOU SAY THE WRONG THING DURING A PRESENTATION**

- **D.O.A.: WHY PRESENTERS HATE BAD INTRODUCTIONS**

- **HANDLING HECKLERS: 5 WAYS THAT PRESENTERS CAN RESTORE ORDER**

Dr. Jim Anderson brings his 25 years of real-world experience to this book. He's delivered speeches at some of the world's largest firms as well as at many conferences. He's going to show you what you need to do in order to make your next speech a success!

www.ingramcontent.com/pod-product-compliance
Lightning Source LLC
Chambersburg PA
CBHW060418190526
45169CB00002B/951